The Summer That Feels Like Winter

But God Changes The Weather

KERRYANN MCBEAN

Copyright © 2025 by .Kerryann Mcbean

All rights reserved. No part of this book may be used or reproduced in any form whatsoever without written permission except in the case of brief quotations in critical articles or reviews.

Printed in the United States of America and or Canada

For more information or to book an event, contact :
info@cojbooz.com

ISBN - Paperback: 978-1-998120-80-2

CONTENTS

Chapter 1 When Warm Days Feel Cold — 2

Chapter 2 The Illusion of Sunshine — 5

Chapter 3 Why Am I Cold in the Heat? — 8

Chapter 4 Unseen Seasons — 11

Chapter 5 When Faith Feels Frozen — 14

Chapter 6 The Forecast Is Not Final — 17

Chapter 7 Delays Are Not Denials — 20

Chapter 8 The Power Of Perserverance — 23

Chapter 9 Thunder & Forgiveness — 26

Chapter 10 The Beauty of Brokenness — 29

Chapter 11 Embracing the Unexpected — 32

Chapter 12 Peace in the Middle — 35

Chapter 13 Strength for the Silent Seasons — 38

Chapter 14 Worship While You Wait — 41

Chapter 15 When Faith Feels Fragile	**44**
Chapter 16 Grace for the Growing	**47**
Chapter 17 Trusting God's Timing	**50**
Chapter 18 When the Breakthrough Comes	**53**
Chapter 19 The Blessing After the Battle	**56**
Chapter 20 The Shift Has Come	**59**
Key Themes & Lessons	**62**
Final Message	**63**

Quote: Sometimes in the brightest season, it feels cold and Joy feels lost, but lift up your eyes to God for season changes, but he stands sure, His words, His Fire —forever sure,
Kerryann Mcbean

CHAPTER 1

When Warm Days Feel Cold

Key Scripture:

"To everything there is a season, and a time for every purpose under heaven."

Ecclesiastes 3:1 (NKJV)

Summer is supposed to feel like joy—bright skies, long days, and a sense of life blooming all around you. But what happens when the calendar says summer, yet your soul feels like winter?

You smile, but it's forced. You show up, but you're numb. You see others flourishing, and you wonder, Why does it feel like I'm the only one frozen in place?

This is the paradox of spiritual seasons: the external doesn't always match the internal. It's entirely possible to walk through a season that looks blessed but feels broken. You can be surrounded by opportunity and still feel empty. You can be in a place of abundance and yet feel like you're starving for peace.

Spiritual winters don't wait for cold months to show up. They hit in the middle of summer barbecues, weddings, job promotions, and baby announcements. You might have everything others are praying for—and still be shivering with sadness, doubt, or confusion.

But here's the truth: God doesn't just show up in springtime joy—He walks into winter too.

He knows what it's like when the heart doesn't match the moment. He understands hidden grief, internal struggle, and the kind of exhaustion that doesn't go away with sleep. And in His love, He's not asking you to fake the season you're in—He's asking you to trust Him in it.

Because even when summer feels like winter, God can still change the weather.

You don't have to force fruit in a frozen place. You don't have to hide your heart behind sunshine-colored posts and perfect Sunday smiles. God wants your real, even if that means offering Him a wintered heart in the heat of July.

This is not denial of reality—it's an invitation to intimacy. Because winter with God is better than summer without Him, when he steps in, He doesn't just bring sunlight—He brings a shift. The kind that doesn't just warm your skin but melts what's been frozen inside of you

Reflection Questions:

1. Have you ever felt emotionally or spiritually cold during a season that should feel joyful?

2. What signs let you know you may be experiencing a spiritual winter?

3. What would it look like to invite God into that space honestly?

Prayer:

Father, I come to You acknowledging that my heart doesn't always match the season I'm in. Even when things look good on the outside, sometimes I'm cold, confused, or hurting within. Thank you for being the God of every season. Help me stop pretending and start trusting. I surrender this inner winter to You and ask You to change the weather within me. In Jesus' name, Amen.

CHAPTER 2

The Illusion of Sunshine

Key Scripture:

"You are like whitewashed tombs, which look beautiful on the outside but on the inside are full of the bones of the dead and everything unclean."

 Matthew 23:27 (NIV)

It's easy to look like you're thriving. You know how to dress the part, say the right things, and post the perfect picture with a well-placed Bible verse. But underneath the layers, there's a chill. A stillness. A soul quietly asking, "Does anyone see the real me?"

This is the illusion of sunshine—the appearance of light when you're secretly surrounded by shadows. You've smiled for so long, even you aren't sure if it's real anymore. You've told yourself, I'm fine—not because it's true, but because it's easier than explaining the cold you're actually carrying.

In a culture that values image, it's tempting to mask your spiritual winters with surface-level warmth. But God never called you to perform joy—He called you to experience it. And true joy doesn't come from performance; it comes from presence—His presence.

God is not impressed by the show. He sees past the sunshine filters and happy captions. He's not afraid of your mess. In fact, He prefers your honest winter to your pretend summer. Because where you're real, He can heal.

Jesus often confronted the illusion of spiritual health. He didn't shame the broken; He challenged the fake. Why? Because pretending delays healing. You can't heal what you refuse to reveal. And sometimes, the very act of removing the mask is what invites the warmth of God's presence to touch the coldest parts of your heart.

What You Must Remember:

•Looking whole is not the same as being whole.

•God doesn't want your perfection—He wants your participation.

•You don't have to fake summer just because everyone else looks like they're in it.

Let God into your winter. Don't dress up the frost with spiritual clichés. He already knows. He's not disappointed—He's ready to do something new. The moment you step out of the illusion, you step into transformation.

Reflection Questions:

1. In what areas of your life have you been "faking the sunshine"?

2. What would it look like to be honest with God and others about where you really are?

3. How has pretending delayed your healing?

Prayer:

Lord, I confess that I've been hiding behind smiles and scriptures, trying to act like I'm okay when I'm not. I don't want to keep pretending. I invite you into the parts of me I've tried to keep polished and presentable. Peel back the layers, and meet me in my truth. Help me be more concerned with your healing than others' opinions. Let your light reach even the parts I've covered. In Jesus' name, Amen.

CHAPTER 3

Why Am I Cold in the Heat?

Key Scripture:

"Yet I hold this against you: You have forsaken the love you had at first."

Revelation 2:4 (NIV)

There are times when life is objectively "good." The bills are paid, you're surrounded by people, and opportunities are open. Yet, deep within, you feel distant. Disconnected. Cold. It's confusing when you're in a season where everything around you says celebrate, but your spirit feels like it's in retreat.

You ask yourself, Why do I feel so far from God? Why does everything feel numb?

That's a question the early church in Ephesus wrestled with. They were doing the right things—serving, working, staying faithful—but they lost something vital along the way: their first love.

You can be spiritually active and emotionally detached. You can be doing church, reading devotions, volunteering, and still feel far from the warmth of God's love. That's not always a sign that something is wrong with your faith; sometimes it means you're being invited to go deeper.

The warmth you're missing isn't found in more work—it's found in more connection. God never created you to live on autopilot. He's not just after your routine; He's after your heart. And when your love for Him cools down, He doesn't punish you—He calls you back.

Think of it this way: when a fire starts to die out, it doesn't mean it's gone. It means it needs tending. That's how it is with your relationship with God. If your fire feels dim, it doesn't mean you've failed—it means you're invited to draw near again.

What You Must Remember:

- Coldness in your spirit is not always sin—it may be distance.

- God will never reject a heart that wants to return.

- Passion isn't always loud—it's consistent.

You don't have to chase a feeling. You just need to return to the flame. Spend time with Him again—not because you "should," but because He's the only one who can warm what's gone cold.

Reflection Questions:

1. Have you felt disconnected from God even when life seems "fine"?

2. What might have contributed to a cooling in your spiritual passion?

3. What steps can you take to return to your first love?

Prayer:

Lord, I confess that I've grown distant. My heart has felt cold, even when everything around me looks good. I don't want to go through the motions—I want my fire for you back. Draw me closer. Teach me how to fall in love with you again. Restore my passion, my intimacy, and my joy in Your presence. In Jesus' name, Amen.

CHAPTER 4

Unseen Seasons

Key Scripture:

"I will give you hidden treasures, riches stored in secret places, so that you may know that I am the Lord, the God of Israel, who summons you by name."

Isaiah 45:3 (NIV

Some of the most powerful seasons of your life won't look like growth. They'll feel silent. Still. Unproductive. You'll look around and wonder, Is anything even happening?

But what you can't see is that God often does His deepest work in the dark.

Just like a seed must go underground before it sprouts, your spirit sometimes enters unseen places so God can strengthen your roots. He's not ignoring you—He's investing in you. In these "winter-like" seasons, God is digging into the foundation of your faith, pulling out what doesn't belong, and quietly developing what will sustain you later.

The world may not celebrate these moments. They don't make for exciting stories or flashy testimonies. But these hidden seasons are holy. Because while the surface seems still, God is moving in secret.

Think about it: when Joseph was thrown into a pit, then a prison, it looked like nothing good was happening. But behind the scenes, God was preparing a palace. When Jesus lay in the tomb, it looked like death had won. But in the unseen realm, resurrection was being written.

Don't rush what God is doing just because it's not visible. Don't mislabel silence as absence. God isn't absent—He's intentional.

What You Must Remember:

•Just because it's quiet doesn't mean it's empty.

•God doesn't waste the hidden places—He uses them to deepen your capacity.

•You are not forgotten. You are being formed.

God is shaping you in secret so He can use you in public. Trust the slow, quiet work. Winter isn't the end—it's preparation for spring.

Reflection Questions:

1. Are you in a season that feels quiet, hidden, or forgotten?

2. What might God be building in you that can't be seen yet?

3. How can you shift your focus from what's missing to what's maturing?

Prayer:

God, thank You for working even when I can't see it. Help me to stop judging this season by what's visible. Teach me to trust the hidden work You're doing in me. Strengthen my roots. Help me believe that silence doesn't mean you're absent. Let this season prepare me for the next one. I trust you in the unseen. In Jesus' name, Amen.

CHAPTER 5

When Faith Feels Frozen

Key Scripture:

"So then faith comes by hearing, and hearing by the word of God."

Romans 10:17 (NKJV)

There are times when faith doesn't feel bold or courageous. It feels frozen.

You believe, but barely. You pray, but the words feel empty. You try to trust, but doubt is louder than truth. You're not denying God—you're just not sure how to keep believing when nothing is changing.

It's in these moments that we discover something powerful about faith: it's not about feelings—it's about focus.

When your faith is frozen, it's often because your hope has been delayed, your prayers seem unanswered, or your expectations have been crushed. The chill sets in slowly, disappointment after disappointment, until you're numb. But God doesn't criticize you for this. Instead, He invites you to reignite your faith, not with hype, but with His Word.

Romans 10:17 tells us that faith doesn't come from wishing or willing—it comes from hearing. That means when your faith is low, the first place to go is His voice, not your feelings. You don't have to feel strong to be strong. You just have to feed your faith.

When everything feels frozen, feed your faith anyway:

•Read the Word, even when it feels dry.

•Speak the truth, even when it feels fake.

•Worship, even when the atmosphere is heavy.

God honors obedience more than emotion. And as you continue to show up, a thaw will begin. Slowly but surely, warmth will return.

What You Must Remember:

•Faith is not the absence of fear or doubt—it's the decision to trust through them.

•Frozen faith is still faith. God can still use it.

•God's Word is the flame that melts the frost around your belief.

You don't need to revive your faith on your own. You just need to give God something to breathe on. Even a small spark is enough for Him to create a fire.

Reflection Questions:

1. Have you ever felt like your faith was frozen or distant?

2. What has been feeding your faith lately, and what has been draining it?

3. How can you realign your focus on God's Word instead of your emotions?

Prayer:

Father, I admit that my faith has felt frozen. I've been tired, disappointed, and numb at times. But I still want you. I still believe—even if it's just a flicker. Help me feed my faith again. Remind me that feelings don't define my relationship with you—faith does. Reignite what has gone cold in me. Let Your Word warm my heart again. In Jesus' name, Amen.

CHAPTER 6

The Forecast Is Not Final

Key Scripture:

"No weapon formed against you shall prosper, and every tongue which rises against you in judgment, you shall condemn. This is the heritage of the servants of the Lord..."

— Isaiah 54:17 (NKJV)

It's easy to believe what you've been told about your future, especially when life keeps reinforcing it. The enemy whispers, "It'll always be like this." People say, "You'll never change." And your own mind starts agreeing, "Maybe this is all there is."

But here's the truth: the forecast over your life is not final unless God said it.

We serve a God who has a history of rewriting the report. Abraham and Sarah were too old. David was too young. Joseph was too rejected. Lazarus was too dead. But none of those "forecasts" stopped the hand of God. And neither will yours.

Maybe the current forecast over your life looks bleak—depression, delay, brokenness, anxiety, grief. But forecasts change. And while the enemy may form weapons and speak curses, Isaiah 54:17 reminds us: they won't prosper.

Why? Because God holds the authority over your life's outcome. He's not confined to the forecast you see today. He's the Changer of conditions, the One who commands the winds, and the Author of your story.

Even if others have tried to label your season, only God has the final say. The enemy may have announced winter, but God still has the power to bring spring.

What You Must Remember:

•The facts may be real, but God's truth is more powerful.

•You are not defined by your diagnosis, situation, or past.

•If God didn't say it, you don't have to accept it.

This chapter of your life is still being written. And the One holding the pen never makes mistakes. Let the enemy forecast whatever he wants. Just remind him: God controls the weather.

Reflection Questions:

1. What negative "forecast" have you been believing about your life or future?

2. How has that belief shaped your faith, your words, or your expectations?

3. What does God's Word say instead—and how can you start speaking that truth daily?

Prayer:

Lord, thank You that no weapon formed against me will prosper. I reject every lie, label, and limitation that others or the enemy have tried to place over my life. I choose to believe your forecast—one of healing, purpose, and peace. Teach me to trust Your Word more than my emotions, reports, or current circumstances. Shift my mindset, and shift my season. In Jesus' name, Amen.

CHAPTER 7

Delays Are Not Denials

Key Scripture:

"The vision is yet for an appointed time... Though it tarries, wait for it; because it will surely come, it will not delay."

— Habakkuk 2:3 (NKJV)

There's a certain weight that comes with waiting. You've prayed. You've believed. You've done everything "right." And yet, nothing seems to be moving. No doors opening. No breakthroughs coming. No answers in sight.

It's in this place that winter winds blow strongest. The cold of delay creeps in, making your heart question, "Did God forget me?"

But hear this clearly: delay does not mean denial.

Just because it hasn't happened yet doesn't mean it's not going to. God is not ignoring you—He's aligning everything in its proper season. When you understand that delay is often part of God's design, you stop viewing it as punishment and start seeing it as preparation.

Sometimes God holds things back—not to withhold, but to refine. He uses delay to:

•Strengthen your trust

•Reveal your motives

- Protect your destiny

- Build your character

If God gave you the promise but not the process, you wouldn't be ready for it. The process of waiting makes room for what you're praying for. What feels like a frozen, inactive season might actually be the most active time spiritually, because God is building you before He brings it.

Think of it this way: winter doesn't cancel spring—it prepares the soil for it.

What You Must Remember:

- Just because it's taking long doesn't mean it's going wrong.

- Waiting seasons are working seasons in God's kingdom.

- God's timing is never late—it's set.

Don't give up because it hasn't happened yet. Stay rooted. Keep praying. Keep expecting. When the appointed time comes, no delay can hold back what God has already declared.

Reflection Questions:

1. What have you been waiting on that's starting to feel like a denial?

2. How might God be preparing you during this delay?

3. What promises can you return to in Scripture to anchor your hope?

Prayer:

Father, I admit that waiting is hard. It challenges my faith and tempts me to doubt. But I choose to believe that you are still working, even in the silence. Remind me that your delays are not rejections—they're redirections. Help me to trust Your timing and stay faithful while I wait. I believe the vision will come, right on time. In Jesus' name, Amen.

CHAPTER 8

The Power of Perseverance

Key Scripture:

"Let us not become weary in doing good, for at the proper time we will reap a harvest if we do not give up."

— Galatians 6:9 (NIV)

The temptation in the middle of a spiritual winter is to quit. The frost feels unbearable. The season feels endless. You want to give up, throw in the towel, and pretend everything is fine. But the Bible makes it clear: You don't get to the harvest without perseverance.

Perseverance isn't just about sticking it out—it's about standing strong through the struggle. It's the choice to keep moving, keep believing, keep working, even when you don't feel the reward. Perseverance says, "I trust the process, even when I can't see the progress."

God never promised that every season would feel like spring. He promised that if we endure, there will be a harvest. That means every prayer prayed, every moment of obedience, every act of faith—it's all going somewhere. Nothing done for God is ever wasted.

In the natural, winter can seem like a season of dormancy. But deep beneath the surface, things are happening. Roots are growing stronger. Nutrients are being gathered. The ground is being prepared for what's coming next. Similarly, your perseverance in spiritual winters is building something you can't yet see, but it will bear fruit in time.

What You Must Remember:

•Perseverance is the key to spiritual growth.

•You may not see the results immediately, but God sees your efforts.

•The harvest is guaranteed—if you don't give up.

Even when the weather doesn't change right away, your obedience is planting seeds for the future. Keep trusting. Keep moving forward. Your breakthrough is coming, but it's found in your perseverance.

Reflection Questions:

1. When was a time you almost gave up, but kept going, and later saw fruit from it?
2. How do you handle seasons where progress feels invisible?
3. How can you grow your perseverance in your current spiritual season?

Prayer:

Lord, You know how hard it can be to keep going when I don't see the results. But I believe you are working even in the unseen. Strengthen my resolve and help me endure. I trust that the harvest will come in due season and that nothing I do in Your name is ever in vain. Give me the perseverance to keep pressing forward, even when the cold feels overwhelming. In Jesus' name, Amen.

CHAPTER 9

Thunder & Forgiveness

Key Scripture:
"For if you forgive other people when they sin against you, your heavenly Father will also forgive you."
 — Matthew 6:14 (NIV)

Some storms in life don't come from circumstances—they come from people.

Words spoken in anger, trust broken, deep disappointments... They rumble through your heart like thunder in a clear sky. Unexpected. Loud. Unsettling.

And like thunder, the echo of those wounds can last long after the storm has passed.

But in the Kingdom, forgiveness is how we clear the skies.

Forgiveness doesn't always feel fair.

It doesn't always feel deserved.

But it's what frees you, not them. It's how you silence the storm on the inside.

God never asks us to ignore the pain, but He does call us to release the offense. Why? Because holding onto bitterness is like standing outside in a thunderstorm, expecting the lightning not to strike. It's dangerous, and it keeps you exposed.

Forgiveness is how you come back under the covering of peace. It doesn't mean the wound didn't happen—it means you trust God to deal with the weight of it.

The thunder may be real, but so is the healing power of grace.

What You Must Remember:

- Forgiveness is not approval—it's release.

- God doesn't ask you to pretend the pain didn't happen; He asks you to trust Him with it.

- When you forgive, you break the power of offense to keep you stuck in a cold season.

The truth is, sometimes your "winter" is extended not because of what happened, but because of what you're still holding. Forgiveness isn't weakness—it's the supernatural strength to move forward without chains.

Reflection Questions:

1. What offense or person still echoes like thunder in your heart?

2. What would it look like to hand that hurt over to God today?

3. Have you fully received God's forgiveness for your own mistakes?

Prayer:

Lord, I've been holding on to things that only You can truly handle. The pain is loud, the betrayal deep—but I don't want to carry this storm anymore. I choose to forgive. Help me to release the offense and trust You to bring justice, healing, and peace. I receive your forgiveness, and I give it away. In Jesus' name, Amen.

CHAPTER 10

The Beauty Of Brokenness

Key Scripture:

"The Lord is near to the brokenhearted and saves those who are crushed in spirit."

— Psalm 34:18 (NIV)

We often avoid brokenness because we associate it with weakness, failure, or even punishment. We pray for God to remove the pain, asking Him to smooth over the jagged edges of our lives. But in God's economy, brokenness has a different purpose.

Brokenness is not the end; it's the beginning of healing.

Think about the most powerful moments in your life—often, they were born out of struggle. The crucifixion of Jesus, the most broken moment in human history, led to the greatest victory ever known. It wasn't the absence of brokenness that brought the resurrection; it was the presence of brokenness and what God did with it.

When you feel broken, it's easy to think you're beyond repair. Yet God specializes in restoration. What the enemy meant for destruction, God uses to create something more beautiful. Broken things in God's hands are not discarded—they are transformed.

Your brokenness does not make you useless; it makes you available for God to do His most beautiful work. Your pain doesn't diminish your value—it makes you relatable. It makes you a vessel of compassion and grace. You can speak into the lives of others in ways that a flawless person never could.

God doesn't waste brokenness. He redeems it. And when He redeems it, the result is something more beautiful than it was before.

What You Must Remember:

- God doesn't break you to destroy you; He breaks you to build you.

- Brokenness in God's hands becomes something new, something whole.

- Your pain has purpose—it's preparing you to carry glory.

God will take your brokenness and craft a masterpiece. Don't shy away from your struggles—let God work in them. Your scars will one day tell a story of healing, hope, and the beauty that only comes through God's hands.

Reflection Questions:

1. How have you seen God use your past brokenness for good in your life or the lives of others?

2. In what ways has your perception of brokenness changed since starting this journey?

3. What areas of your life do you still struggle to surrender to God for healing?

Prayer:

Lord, thank You that You are near to the brokenhearted. I surrender my brokenness to You, knowing that You can heal and redeem it. I trust that you will not waste my pain, but that you will make something beautiful from it. Heal the wounds in my heart, and use my story to bring comfort and hope to others. In Jesus' name, Amen.

CHAPTER 11

Embracing the Unexpected

Key Scripture:

"For My thoughts are not your thoughts, neither are your ways My ways," declares the Lord. "As the heavens are higher than the earth, so are My ways higher than your ways and My thoughts than your thoughts."

— Isaiah 55:8-9 (NIV)

There's an old saying, "Expect the unexpected." It's one of those phrases that sounds simple, but carries a deep truth: life is rarely what we expect it to be. We make plans, set goals, and chart courses, but the unexpected often knocks on the door.

The problem with the unexpected is that it's often uncomfortable. When things go differently than we imagined, it can feel like a setback. A detour. A disruption to everything we thought we knew. But in God's economy, the unexpected is often where He does His most profound work.

Think about the life of Jesus. Time and time again, He stepped into situations that were unexpected. He was born in a manger, not a palace. He healed on the Sabbath, shocking the religious leaders. He associated with the outcasts of society, defying cultural expectations. His death on the cross was the most unexpected event in all of history, but it led to the greatest victory of all.

In the same way, God often disrupts our plans because He has something better in mind. We can't always understand why things happen the way they do, but we can trust that God's ways are higher than ours (Isaiah 55:9). When we embrace the unexpected, we make room for the extraordinary.

It's in these unexpected moments where we often find God's presence the most profound. When life shakes us from our comfort zones, it's an invitation to trust in a way that goes beyond our plans, our understanding, and our control.

The unexpected is not something to fear—it's something to embrace. It's where the miracles happen, the breakthroughs unfold, and the beauty of God's plan is revealed.

What You Must Remember:

- God is not surprised by your circumstances—He has a plan, even in the unexpected.

- The unexpected can be the space where God works in ways you never imagined.

- Trusting God means letting go of your own plans and embracing His.

Sometimes the very thing you thought was a detour is actually the road you needed to be on. The unexpected is not an interruption; it's a divine invitation to see God at work in new and exciting ways.

Reflection Questions:

1. What unexpected events in your life have challenged or changed you the most?

2. How do you typically react when things don't go according to your plans?

3. In what areas of your life do you need to release control and trust God with the unexpected?

Prayer:

Father, I admit that I struggle with the unexpected. It challenges my plans, my comfort, and my expectations. But I trust that Your ways are higher than mine. Help me to embrace the unexpected with faith, knowing that You are working even in the things I don't understand. Teach me to trust You more deeply and surrender my plans to You. In Jesus' name, Amen.

CHAPTER 12

Peace In The Middle

Key Scripture:

"You will keep in perfect peace all who trust in You, all whose thoughts are fixed on You!"

— Isaiah 26:3 (NLT)

One of the greatest lies the enemy whispers during difficult seasons is this: "You'll only have peace when this is over."

But that's not the kind of peace God offers.

God doesn't promise peace after the storm—He offers peace in the middle of it.

It's easy to believe that peace only comes when problems are solved, when prayers are answered, or when life finally goes the way you want. But if that's the only peace you know, it's not lasting. It's conditional peace. Temporary peace. Circumstantial peace.

God, however, gives us perfect peace—not because everything is right around us, but because we're aligned with the One who holds everything together. Isaiah 26:3 tells us this kind of peace is available to "all who trust in You... all whose thoughts are fixed on You."

It doesn't say your peace is based on a perfect situation—it says it's based on your focus.

When you shift your eyes from the storm to the Savior, peace is possible. When you stop meditating on what's missing and start meditating on Who's present, peace becomes your reality—even if nothing else has changed.

Peace is not the absence of trouble. It's the presence of God in the middle of it.

What You Must Remember:

•Peace is not found in the outcome; it's found in your focus.

•You can be in the fire and still be calm—when God is in the fire with you.

•The storm around you does not have to become a storm within you.

Your situation doesn't have to be perfect for your spirit to be still. Peace isn't postponed—it's available now. And God is faithful to guard your heart and mind when you set your eyes on Him.

Reflection Questions:

1. What area of your life feels stormy or chaotic right now?

2. What have you been focusing on—your problem, or God's presence?

3. What practices (prayer, worship, stillness) can help you cultivate peace in this season?

Prayer:

Lord, thank You that You offer perfect peace, not because of my circumstances, but because of who You are. Teach me to fix my mind on You. Help me not to chase peace in temporary things, but to root myself in Your presence. Calm the storm inside me, even if the storm outside remains. I trust that you are with me in the middle. In Jesus' name, Amen.

CHAPTER 13

Strength For The Silent Seasons

Key Scripture:

"But those who wait on the Lord shall renew their strength; they shall mount up with wings like eagles, they shall run and not be weary, they shall walk and not faint."

 Isaiah 40:31 (NKJV)

There's a certain kind of difficulty that comes not from chaos, but from silence.

You pray, but there's no response.

You seek, but nothing shifts.

You show up, but Heaven seems quiet.

These are the silent seasons—when it feels like God has stepped back, and you're left in the stillness, wondering if He's even paying attention.

But silence is not absence. God is still near. He's just teaching you to hear Him in a deeper way.

Sometimes God quiets the noise around you so you can learn to trust what He already told you. He's not always going to repeat the promise—sometimes, He wants you to walk on the last Word He gave you.

Isaiah 40:31 reminds us that those who wait on the Lord will renew their strength. That word "wait" isn't passive—it means to expect, hope, lean into, and bind yourself to God. Silent seasons are when you learn not to rely on feelings but on faith. You grow not through noise, but through nourishment in His presence.

In the silence, He's strengthening your roots.

In the silence, He's preparing your wings.

In the silence, He's renewing your strength so you can rise again.

What You Must Remember:

- God's silence is not a sign of His absence—it's often a setup for strength.

- You don't have to feel God to know He's working.

- Waiting on the Lord brings supernatural renewal—not just survival, but strength.

The silence isn't wasted. It's sacred. Stay close. Stay faithful. The next Word is coming—but in the meantime, your strength is being restored.

Reflection Questions:

1. Have you ever experienced a season where God felt silent? How did you respond?

2. What can you do during the silent seasons to stay spiritually nourished?

3. How does Isaiah 40:31 encourage you in your current waiting or silence?

Prayer:

Father, I admit that silence can feel heavy. It makes me question, fear, and doubt. But I choose to trust that You are working even when I cannot hear You. Strengthen me as I wait. Help me to hope, expect, and cling to You, even in stillness. I believe you are preparing me to rise again—stronger, wiser, and more faithful. In Jesus' name, Amen.

CHAPTER 14

Worship While You Wait

Key Scripture:

"About midnight, Paul and Silas were praying and singing hymns to God, and the other prisoners were listening to them. Suddenly, there was such a violent earthquake that the foundations of the prison were shaken."

Acts 16:25–26 (NIV)

Waiting seasons often come with pressure: pressure to fix things, pressure to figure things out, pressure to escape. But sometimes the most powerful thing you can do in a season of uncertainty is this: worship.

In Acts 16, Paul and Silas were in a place no one would envy—beaten, chained, and imprisoned for doing the will of God. But instead of complaining or collapsing under the weight of their circumstance, they did something supernatural—they worshiped.

They didn't wait for freedom to come to worship; they worshiped while they were still bound.

That's the power of praise.

It doesn't deny what's happening—it defies it.

It doesn't ignore the pain—it invites God into it.

It turns a prison into a platform for a miracle.

God responds to praise because praise shifts the atmosphere. It reminds you of who God is, not just what you feel. It lifts your focus off the chains and back onto the Chain-Breaker.

And here's the key: the earthquake didn't come before the worship—it came after. That tells us something powerful: breakthrough often follows worship, not the other way around.

So when you're in a cold, stagnant, or confusing season, worship anyway. Sing through your sorrow. Praise through your pressure. Declare God's goodness when everything else feels bad.

Because worship doesn't just move Heaven—it changes you.

What You Must Remember:

- Worship is a weapon, especially in waiting seasons.

- You don't worship because of how things feel—you worship because of who God is.

- Praise in the prison leads to freedom on the other side.

Even when the answers haven't come and the season hasn't changed, God is still worthy. And when you worship in the winter, you invite the warmth of His presence right where you are.

Reflection Questions:

1. How do you normally respond in seasons of waiting or disappointment?

2. What would it look like to worship God fully, even before you see the breakthrough?

3. What songs, scriptures, or declarations help shift your atmosphere when life feels heavy?

Prayer:

God, even when I don't understand my situation, I choose to worship You. I declare that you are good, faithful, and in control, no matter what I feel. Help me to lift my eyes from my circumstances and fix them on You. Teach me to praise You while I wait, and let my worship be a testimony of trust. In Jesus' name, Amen.

CHAPTER 15

When Faith Feels Fragile

Key Scripture:

"I do believe; help me overcome my unbelief!"

Mark 9:24 (NIV)

There are times when your faith doesn't feel bold. It doesn't sound loud. It doesn't walk confidently.

It trembles.

It questions.

It wonders if it's even real.

If you've ever felt that way, welcome to the human experience. Even the greatest men and women of faith had moments where belief collided with doubt.

In Mark 9, a desperate father brought his suffering son to Jesus. He wanted to believe that healing was possible, but doubt still lingered in his heart. His confession is one of the most honest in all of Scripture: "I do believe; help my unbelief."

Jesus didn't reject him. He didn't scold him for having questions. He responded with compassion, and He healed the boy anyway.

This shows us something important: God isn't threatened by your fragile faith.

In fact, He meets you in it.

God doesn't need you to have perfect faith; He needs you to have present faith. Just enough to bring what you have—even if it's broken, bruised, or barely holding on.

Faith isn't the absence of doubt—it's the decision to keep going, even when doubt whispers loudly.

What You Must Remember:

- God honors honest faith—even when it's shaky.

- You don't have to feel strong to be strong in the Spirit.

- What matters most is not the size of your faith, but the object of your faith.

Don't disqualify yourself because your faith feels fragile. The fact that you're still showing up, still seeking, still praying—that's faith in motion. And God can move mountains with faith the size of a mustard seed.

Reflection Questions:

1. What situations in your life have tested your faith the most?

2. Have you ever felt like your belief and unbelief existed at the same time?

3. How can you invite God into your doubts rather than hide them?

Prayer:

God, sometimes my faith feels small. I believe—but I also struggle. Thank you for not turning away from me when I doubt, but drawing me closer. Help me trust You in the middle of uncertainty. Strengthen what feels weak in me, and remind me that You are still faithful, even when I am fragile. In Jesus' name, Amen.

CHAPTER 16

Grace for the Growing

Key Scripture:

"He who began a good work in you will carry it on to completion until the day of Christ Jesus."

Philippians 1:6 (NIV)

Growth doesn't always look graceful.

Sometimes it's messy, awkward, and slow.

It's two steps forward, one step back. It's blooming in one area and still battling weeds in another. But the beauty of spiritual growth is that God gives grace for every part of it.

We live in a world that glorifies instant results. But God's process is often gradual. He's not just after your destination—He's after your development. He's more concerned with who you're becoming than how fast you're getting there.

It's easy to grow frustrated with yourself when you feel like you should be further along. Maybe you're tired of the same struggle resurfacing or ashamed of how long healing is taking. But here's the truth: God is patient with your progress, so you should be too.

Philippians 1:6 reminds us that the good work God started in you isn't finished yet. You're a work in progress, and progress is still progress, even if it's slow.

Stop disqualifying yourself because you're not perfect. Growth means you're still in it. You're still showing up. You're still learning. And God is still working.

What You Must Remember:

•Growth is not always visible, but it is always valuable.

•You are not a finished product, but you are God's ongoing masterpiece.

•Give yourself grace, because God already has.

The same God who started your story is committed to finishing it. You don't have to strive to be perfect—just keep surrendering and trusting the process. Grace covers every gap.

Reflection Questions:

1. In what areas of your life have you grown, even if just a little?

2. Where are you being hard on yourself for not being "there" yet?

3. What would it look like to give yourself the same grace God gives you?

Prayer:

Lord, thank You for being patient with me. Thank you for not rushing my process or giving up on me when I stumble. Remind me that growth takes time and that you are with me in every stage. Help me to receive Your grace and extend it to myself. I trust that what You've started in me, You will finish. In Jesus' name, Amen.

CHAPTER 17

Trusting God's Timing

Key Scripture:

"He has made everything beautiful in its time."

 Ecclesiastes 3:11 (NIV)

One of the hardest things to surrender is control over timing.

We want it now—answers, healing, breakthrough, change. And when it doesn't happen on our schedule, frustration builds. We wonder if God heard us. If he cares. If he's forgotten.

But God's timing is not random—it's perfect.

Ecclesiastes 3:11 assures us that God makes all things beautiful in His time. That doesn't mean your waiting is wasted. It means there is a divine rhythm behind every delay.

What feels like a pause to you may be God protecting, preparing, or positioning you.

He's not just lining up circumstances—He's aligning your heart. Because sometimes, if God gave us what we wanted too soon, we wouldn't be ready to handle it.

Think about it: premature blessings can become burdens if received outside of purpose. But blessings that come in God's timing are marked by peace, clarity, and sustainability.

So what do you do while you wait?

Trust.

Trust that God sees the full picture. Trust that He's never late. Trust that even the delays are part of the design.

Because when His timing unfolds, it doesn't just fulfill your hopes—it reveals His glory.

What You Must Remember:

- God's timing is not just about delay—it's about divine development.

- Waiting doesn't mean nothing is happening. God is always working behind the scenes.

- What God makes beautiful, He makes on time—never too early, never too late.

Even in the seasons that feel long and uncertain, He is on schedule. You can trust His pace, even when it doesn't match your preference.

Reflection Questions:

1. In what area of your life are you currently struggling to trust God's timing?

2. How has God's past timing proven better than your own plans?

3. What do you sense God might be preparing you for in the waiting?

Prayer:

Father, I confess that waiting is hard. It tests my patience and my trust. But today, I surrender the clock. I believe that you know the best time for everything in my life. Help me not to rush what you are refining. Teach me to rest in Your timing, knowing that what You're preparing is worth the wait. In Jesus' name, Amen.

CHAPTER 18

When the Breakthrough Comes

Key Scripture:

"The Lord has done great things for us, and we are filled with joy."

Psalm 126:3 (NIV)

After the tears, the tests, the trials, and the waiting, breakthrough comes.

Maybe not the way you expected. Maybe not in the timing you hoped. But when God moves, it's unmistakable.

It shifts everything. And suddenly, the cold season you've endured starts to feel the warmth of change.

Psalm 126 speaks of a people who had been in captivity, crying out for deliverance. When God finally restored them, it felt like a dream. Their mouths were filled with laughter. Their hearts were flooded with joy. And everyone around them took notice—"The Lord has done great things for them."

That's what a breakthrough does.

It reminds you of God's faithfulness.

It restores what was lost.

It renews your joy.

But here's what's just as important: breakthrough doesn't mean the process was pointless. The waiting, the pruning, the stretching—it all had purpose. The winter prepared you for the harvest. The valley made you appreciate the mountaintop.

Breakthrough isn't just about what God gives—it's about what He's done in you.

It makes you stronger.

More grateful.

More sensitive to His voice.

More rooted in His love.

The fruit you see now came from seeds you planted in faith, tears you cried in silence, and prayers you whispered when you didn't think they were being heard.

What You Must Remember:

- Breakthrough isn't the end—it's a reflection of God's faithfulness.

- Every season of pain had purpose. Nothing was wasted.

- When God restores, He always adds more than what was lost.

So when the breakthrough comes, don't forget to give Him glory. Celebrate. Testify. Rejoice. Because this isn't just a change of circumstances—it's a testimony of God's power to change everything.

Reflection Questions:

1. Has God brought you through something that once felt impossible?

2. What did the waiting season teach you that you're thankful for now?

3. How can you share your breakthrough as an encouragement to others?

Prayer:

God, thank You for breakthrough. Thank you for showing me that the season I thought would last forever was preparing me for this moment. Help me never forget where You brought me from. Give me the boldness to testify, to celebrate, and to worship with joy. I give you all the glory. In Jesus' name, Amen.

CHAPTER 19

The Blessing After The Battle

Key Scripture:

"After Job had prayed for his friends, the Lord restored his fortunes and gave him twice as much as he had before."

Job 42:10 (NIV)

Every battle leaves marks. Some visible. Some invisible. But when you walk with God, every scar tells a story of survival, and every story leads to restoration.

Job lost everything: family, wealth, health, and the respect of those around him. His winter wasn't just cold—it was crushing. Yet by the end of his story, after all the pain and questions, Scripture says God restored Job's fortunes and gave him double what he had before.

But the blessing didn't come instead of the battle—it came after it.

Too often, we want the reward without the resistance. But in the Kingdom, battles refine you. They develop you. And God uses them to usher you into deeper levels of blessing, character, and understanding.

Notice this too: Job's restoration came after he prayed for others, even those who had misunderstood him. That's not just a detail—it's a lesson. Forgiveness often unlocks favor.

The blessing wasn't just material—it was spiritual. Job walked away with a new revelation of who God is. And that kind of knowing—born through suffering and sustained by faith—is more valuable than anything the world can offer.

What You Must Remember:

- The blessing isn't proof that the battle didn't happen—it's proof that God brought you through it.

- God often gives double for your trouble—not just to restore, but to redeem.

- Sometimes the biggest breakthrough comes when you release what hurts you.

The storm you survived didn't break you. It built you. And now, what God is bringing into your life will testify that you're not just healed—you're whole.

Reflection Questions:

1. What battles have shaped you the most in this season?

2. Have you experienced restoration in an area that once felt lost?

3. Who might you need to release or forgive so that you can fully walk into your blessing?

Prayer:

Lord, thank You for being the God who restores. I may have lost some things in the storm, but I've gained something greater—faith, strength, and deeper trust in You. Help me walk in the blessing with humility and gratitude. Teach me to forgive freely, so nothing blocks what You have for me. In Jesus' name, Amen.

CHAPTER 20

The Shift Has Come

Key Scripture:

"See, I am doing a new thing! Now it springs up; do you not perceive it?"

Isaiah 43:19 (NIV)

There comes a moment when the atmosphere changes.

The weight lifts.

The cold starts to fade.

And you realize—the season has shifted.

You're no longer surviving- you're thriving.

No longer wandering... you're walking with direction.

What once felt like endless winter now carries the evidence of new life, new strength, and new beginnings.

That's what God does.

He doesn't just end the storm. He births something fresh through it.

He doesn't just stop the suffering. He revives what was buried beneath it.

He doesn't just change your surroundings. He transforms you.

Isaiah 43:19 isn't just a verse about what God might do—it's a declaration of what He is doing. Right now. In your heart, in your life, and in your purpose. The shift has come—not just in weather, but in worship, wisdom, and identity.

You've learned to trust in the silence.

You've learned to praise in the pain.

You've grown roots in dry ground.

And now... you're ready for the rain.

You didn't just endure a hard season—you walked with God through it. And because of that, this next season will be marked not by loss, but by life.

What You Must Remember:

• The shift isn't just external—it's internal. You've changed.

God uses every season to prepare you for what's next.

• When the shift comes, walk boldly. Don't look back—move forward in faith.

This is the new thing God has been working on behind the scenes all along. It may have felt like winter, but the shift in the spirit has already begun. God changed the weather. And he changed you, too.

Reflection Questions:

1. Looking back, how has God shifted your mindset, your heart, or your faith through this season?

2. What new thing is God doing in you that you're ready to embrace?

3. How can you walk into this new season with boldness and joy?

Prayer:

God, thank You for bringing me through the season that felt like winter. I see now that you were with me all along—working, shaping, strengthening. I received the new thing you're doing. Help me walk in it with faith, courage, and gratitude. I declare that this is a new season, and I step into it with expectation. In Jesus' name, Amen.

Key Themes & Lessons:

1. Spiritual Seasons Exist — Even in your "summer," life may feel cold. God still works in off-seasons.

2. Faith in the Fog — Trusting God when you can't see what He's doing sharpens your spiritual vision.

3. Purpose in the Pain — God doesn't waste anything; your struggle is shaping your story.

4. Healing Takes Time — Growth is often invisible before it's impactful. Let grace meet you in the process.

5. Praise is Power — Worship in the middle of the storm shifts your focus and welcomes breakthrough.

6. God's Timing is Perfect — Delays are not denials. Trust the process and the One guiding it.

7. Breakthrough Comes After — After the tears, after the pressing, then comes the release.

8. Restoration is Real — What felt lost can be restored by God, often with double the blessing.

9. The Shift Happens Inside First — Your heart shifts before your circumstances do. That's where real change begins.

10. You Were Never Alone — Through every winter-feeling season, God was always right there, working on your behalf.

Final Message:

The weather may have felt like winter, but God was changing the climate of your life the whole time.

Now that the shift has come, it's time to walk forward in joy, boldness, and faith, fully alive in the new season God has prepared for you.

God Remnant Mcbean♥

The Summer That Feels Like Winter, But God Changes The Weather

www.ingramcontent.com/pod-product-compliance
Lightning Source LLC
Chambersburg PA
CBHW070921180426
43192CB00038B/2148